101 FUNNY THINGS ABOUT GLOBAL WARMING

BY THE SAME AUTHOR

101 FUNNY THINGS ABOUT GLOBAL WARMING

Sidney Harris & Colleagues

BLOOMSBURY

Published by Bloomsbury USA, New York
Distributed to the trade by Macmillan

All papers used by Bloomsbury USA are natural, recyclable products made
from wood grown in well-managed forests. The manufacturing processes conform
to the environmental regulations of the country of origin.

LIBRARY OF CONGRESS CATALOGING-IN-PUBLICATION DATA HAS BEEN APPLIED FOR.

ISBN-10 1-59691-482-3
ISBN-13 978-1-59691-482-7

First U.S. Edition 2008

1 3 5 7 9 10 8 6 4 2

Designed by Marina Drukman
Printed in the United States of America by Quebecor World Fairfield

CONTRIBUTORS

MATT DIFFEE

NICK DOWNES

JOSEPH FARRIS

ED FRASCINO

FELIPE GALINDO (FEGGO)

MORT GERBERG

SAM GROSS

TOM HACHTMAN

SIDNEY HARRIS

PAUL KANE

BEN KATCHOR

GLENN LE LIEVRE

LEE LORENZ

HUGUETTE MARTEL

ED McLACHLAN

WARREN MILLER

DAN PIRARO

BOB WEBER

MIKE WILLIAMS

GAHAN WILSON

JACK ZIEGLER

"You'll knock 'em dead on the red carpet and save the planet.
It's made entirely from recycled garbage."

"Hot enough for ya?"

"Sorry I'm late, but I'm actually driving one of these things."

"...moreover, I have personally signed the Kyoto Protocol."

"Now let them talk about us using private jets."

"In addition to the wind turbines and the solar panels,
it features a new technology that separates the
good hydrocarbons from the bad hydrocarbons."

"We'll have to start looking at senior citizens homes. There's not enough ice these days to float Grandma."

"…and you can eat the containers."

Huguette Martel

"It recharges my iPod."

"This is the first time we've met the directors of our main supplier so we need to make sure we make a good impression."

LEE IACOCCA —
AUTOMOTIVE EXECUTIVE

"And do you promise to honor the environment and live green?"

LAND CLEARED
FOR
WORLD HEADQUARTERS
RAIN FOREST
PRESERVATION
INSTITUTE

JAMES WATT – U.S.
SECRETARY OF THE INTERIOR

"'Just imagine!' said The Little SUV Engine. 'If I could increase my mileage efficiency by only three miles per gallon…'"

"Global warming's coming and I haven't a thing to wear."

"There—a tree! Now let's hear the environment people complain."

EL NIÑO AND LA NIÑA AT HOME
(OFF SEASON)

MARGARET THATCHER –
BRITISH PRIME MINISTER

"The cash assets go to his alma mater, but the carbon credits are divided equally among the family."

"They asked about how we live, took some pictures, congratulated us for a lot of things we don't do, and left."

"Regrettably, your home-owner policy does not cover melting."

"The Abominable Snowman is up there with his beach
chair and umbrella, trying to cool off."

"I've had enough! I'm going to try another car pool."

SATAN ATTEMPTS TO REDIRECT THE CHURCH'S PRIMARY FOCUS FROM EVANGELISM TO ENVIRONMENTALISM.

JERRY FALWELL - EVANGELIST

"They say it's a bad sign when the pigeons are coughing."

"I can't stop worrying about anthropogenic influence on nature."

"I like corn the way it is, so I sure hope they
don't start forcing ethanol on us."

"Because of plants like ours, the USA is number one in the world, emitting more carbon dioxide into the atmosphere than China, India and Japan combined."

"I use my microwave—faster, easier, and *no carbon*."

GLOBAL WARMING REACHES HÄAGEN-DAZS HILL

In The Shade by Ben Katchor

THOSE INDIVIDUALS WHO ARE MOST SENSITIVE TO THE RAYS OF THE SUN...

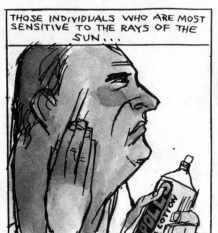

WALK, WHENEVER POSSIBLE, ON THE SHADY SIDE OF THE STREET.

ONE HALF OF THE CITY REMAINS OUT OF THEIR REACH FOR PART OF THE DAY.

I'LL PICK UP MY JACKET IN THE AFTERNOON.

MAEST
DRY CLEA

AS NOON APPROACHES, THEY'RE FORCE TO CLING TO THE NARROW SHADOWS CAST BY OVERHANGING DETAILS OF 19th AND EARLY 20th CENTURY BUILDINGS.

SAVINGS

NOW SERVES A GRIM PURPOSE.

BULBOUS MOLDINGS, BAY WINDOWS...

ONE MAN GOES SEVERAL BLOCKS OUT OF HIS WAY TO AVOID THE SUN.

PEDIMENTS AND DRIPSTONES

HIS LEATHER SHOES ARE SCUFFED AGAINST STONE.

LINTELS AND BALUSTRADES.

NEWER BUILDINGS, WITH THEIR SHEER, UNBROKEN FACADES, ARE OF NO HELP.

THE BUS-STOP SIGNS HAVE BEEN BLEACHED INTO ILLEGIBILITY.

PEOPLE SMELL OF SUNTAN LOTION ALL YEAR ROUND.

A DERMATOLOGIST WATCHES FROM HIS OFFICE WINDOW...

AS A MAN DARTS FROM ONE BIT OF SHADE TO ANOTHER.

"We're leaving. They allow smoking in the parking lot."

"I don't give advice. I'm only up here because it's safer."

"It's another buyout proposal, Mother Nature,
and they're really quite insistent!"

"Since we moved to the country, William and I have gone totally green, living off the land and being total vegetarians."

"When I think of all this sunshine going to waste..."

"Thank goodness it's wet heat."

"Never mind the delicate balance of nature—what about
the delicate balance of business and finance?"

"The end of life on earth as I've known it wouldn't be such a tragedy."

"Solar heat is fine but I miss our privacy."

"This is just like home—the martians dumping
industrial wastes into their fabled canals."

"There! Do you still believe global warming is a myth?"

"We tried solar, we tried wind, and now we have
a little nuclear reactor out back."

"Best of all, it's made from 100% recycled materials."

"Rupert Murdoch is saying global warming is real. I guess maybe we should move to a higher ground now."

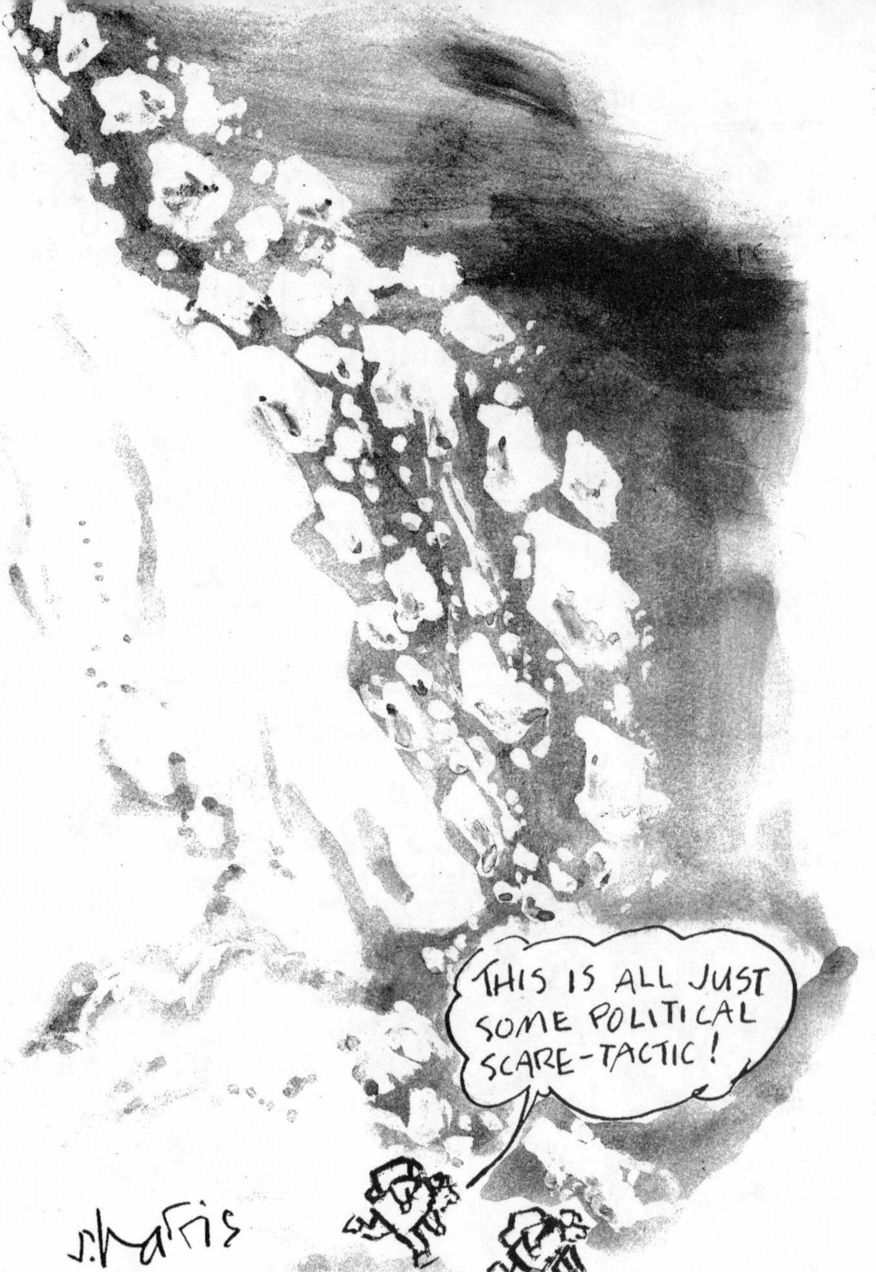
THIS IS ALL JUST SOME POLITICAL SCARE-TACTIC!
J. Marris

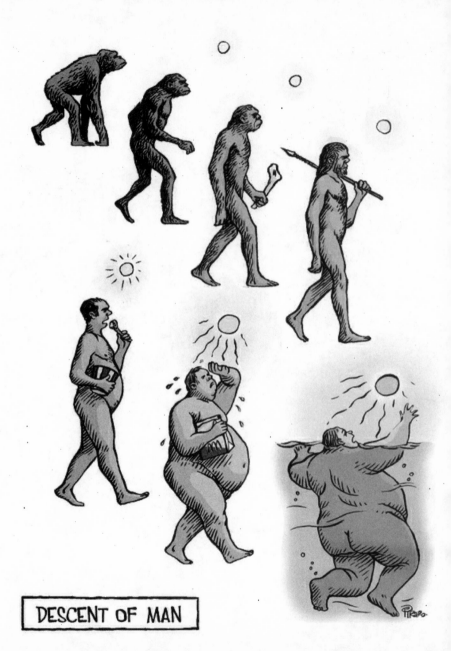

DESCENT OF MAN

PAT BUCHANAN —
POLITICAL COMMENTATOR

"Oh, for heaven's sake—you blame everything on global warming."

"Some do their part by planting trees. We decided to raise Fanto."

THE TIP OF THE ICEBERG (ALL THAT'S LEFT.)

MAY OR MAY NOT BE
HAZARDOUS MATERIAL
DEPENDING ON WHETHER
YOU FOLLOW
INTERNATIONAL, NATIONAL,
LOCAL OR INDUSTRY
GUIDELINES
S. Harris

"There's a polar bear in the garbage over on West Bluebird Lane."

DICK CHENEY —
U.S. VICE PRESIDENT

I'm just so worried about mercury in the water and sulfur dioxide in the air.
GROUNDLESS FEARS, NOT WORTH YOUR TIME. IT'S THE DEAD ZONES IN THE OCEAN CAUSED BY ALGAE, AND CARBON PARTICLES IN THE AIR WHICH SHOULD BE TERRIFYING YOU.
S. Harris

"Six gallons of ethanol, three of it corn, two of it
sugar cane and the rest cellulosic biomass."

"Yes, this certainly is a highly polluted piece of air."

"…And most important, how large is your carbon footprint?"

"A great fighter for the environment, right to the very end."

"The seas will rise in three-to-six years!
The seas will rise in three-to-six years!"

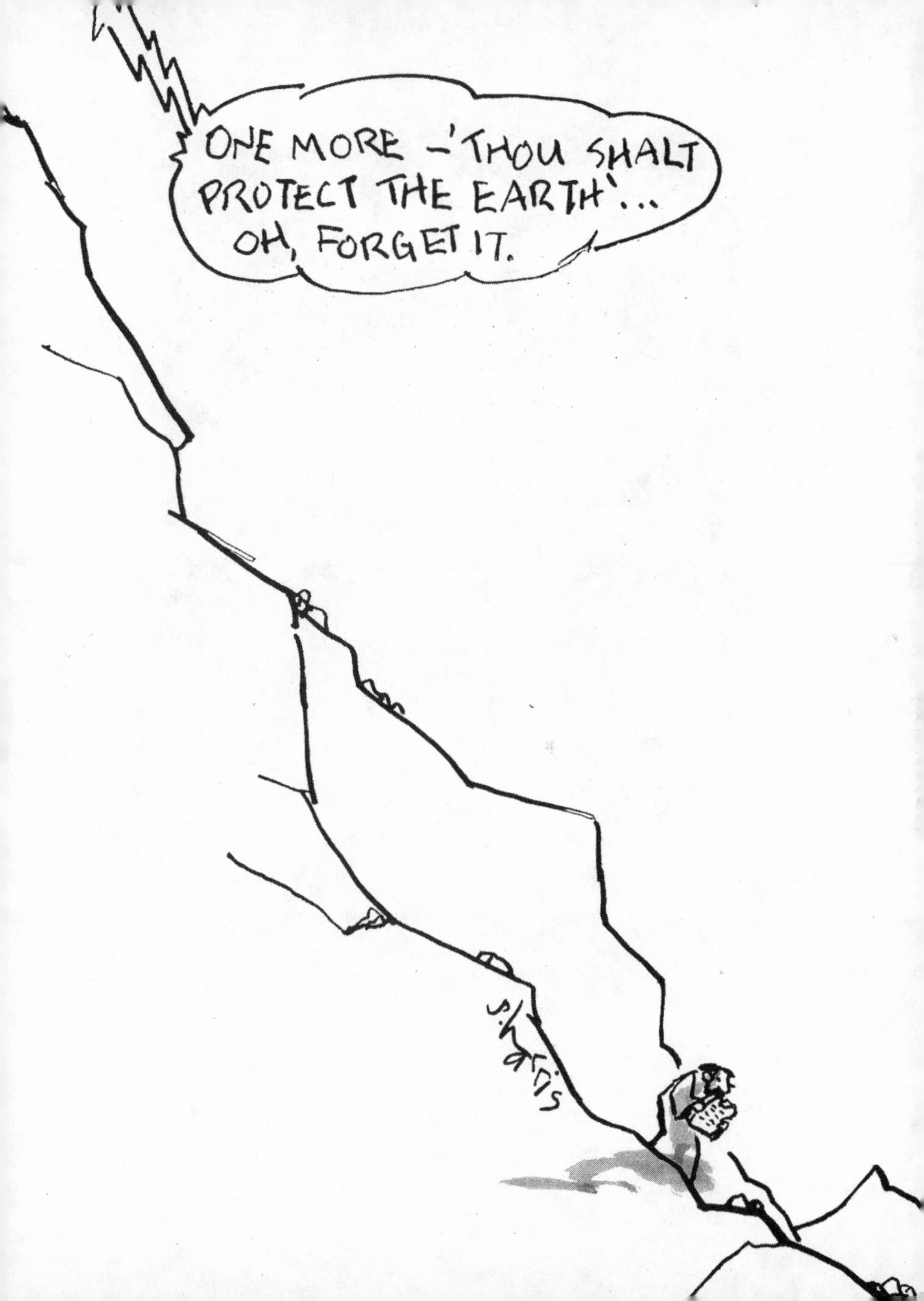
ONE MORE – 'THOU SHALT PROTECT THE EARTH'... OH, FORGET IT.
S. Harris

"The President very strongly feels that all knowledge of this satellite image be strictly confined to ourselves and the other folks here at the project."